A-Z OF MY LIFE

PIYUSH PADWALE

Made with ♥ on the Notion Press Platform
www.notionpress.com

Here's to my creator and source of inspiration,

who never stop believing in me.

Contents

Contents

Acknowledgements

This is my first English book, and first and foremost, I'd like to thank my parents for their unwavering support. I'm deeply grateful to my family members and friends who have always stood by me, recognized my passions, and encouraged me to pursue them.

A special mention to Notion Press Publishing for providing me with this platform to share my expressions with the world. They've been instrumental in bringing this book to life.

And finally, to all my lovely readers—thank you for taking the time to explore my writings. If I've managed to impact your life, even in the smallest way, that means the world to me. I hope to continue spreading joy, hope, and carving a small space for myself in your hearts.

Preface

I started writing at the tender age of 16, with my first piece dedicated to my mother on the occasion of Mother's Day. It was well received, and I realized I had found a heartfelt and expressive skill through which I could wholeheartedly express myself.

Naturally, as time passed and life unfolded, writing took a backseat when I entered college to pursue my bachelor's degree in architecture. That was until a close person in my life urged me to write something for my senior's farewell during their graduation. This moment marked a significant turning point, as, after nearly five years, I rediscovered my passion for writing, and since then, there's been no looking back.

I began exploring themes of love, life, and personal experiences, writing whenever inspiration struck. Slowly, I found myself collecting a wide range of pieces, and I felt that they needed to be shared with the public. My hope is that through recognizing my work, I can have an impact on lives and instill feelings of hope and optimism in people's hearts and minds.

I truly believe that, over time, due to the nature of life and its rigid structure, people often lose touch with themselves. They surrender to societal norms without taking a moment to reflect and truly experience the joys of life. Through my work, I hope to inspire others to recognize and fuel their happiness, purpose, and ultimately help them rediscover the real them.

That is what has ultimately led to the creation of this book—with the hope that in the process of you getting to know me, you will also discover yourself.

Contents

CONTENTS

1. Aim, Aspire, Achieve

"Chasing dreams, no matter how far, with the fire of desire to take me where I belong."

No matter how lame,
But always have a big aim.
There aren't rules to this game,
Anything and everything you do,
Just adds to making your name.
All that you aspire,
Is just another step to inspire,
Building up a flame of desire,
This is the kind of fulfilment,
I wish to acquire.
Maybe too hard to believe,
And sometimes too late to receive,
But come what may,
I'll never be far from,
The things I want to achieve.

2. Believe, Build, Become

"Embrace the journey, trust the process, and let your dreams lead you to where you truly belong."

It's time to roll up your sleeve,
Irrespective of the outcome,
Just believe.
Even if it feels like delusion,
Never stop to perceive.
Make yourself strong,
Know this is where you belong.
Lead a life that feels fulfilled,
That's when happiness you shall build.
Become what you feel inside,
Let dreams, and reality collide.
The journey's a beautiful ride,
And when you reach where you long to be,
You'll know it was the perfect stride.

3. Create, Chase, Conquer

"Create without fear, chase with grace—your spark will always find its place."

When ideas come in straight,
You know it's time to create.
It's never too early or too late,
To find that one thing
You can truly relate.
Transitioning into a beautiful phase,
Even in this never-ending race,
You somehow embrace the chase,
With a bright smile on your face.
Never shy away to discover,
It's your unique power.
Wherever you place your anchor,
You shall always conquer.

4. Dream, Decide, Deliver

"Where imagination flows and dreams take shape—your vision,
your path, your triumph to create."

Imagination is a theme,
With thoughts flowing down the stream.
But the ones that keep you afloat
That, my friend,
Is your special dream.
A place where your vision resides,
Where different paths may collide.
Even then, it's only you
Who gets to decide
Who earns a share of the outcome,
Without a divide.
When hard work, persistence,
And dedication are in order,
Success, peace, and happiness
Will surely deliver.

5. Excite, Establish, Entertain

"Chasing dreams not for gain, but to spark joy—even if it means turning my pain into someone else's smile."

Keep your dreams and vision in sight,
It doesn't matter
If it's wrong or right,
As long as you're the one
Who feels the excite.
Work hard and cherish,
It will take time,
But what's yours
Will never vanish.
One day, you will establish.
The goal is clear,
I just want to entertain,
To create moments where people
Forget their fears,
Even at the cost of my pain.

6. Faith, Focus, Fulfill

"Let faith be your fuel, focus your fire—only you can turn doubt into undeniable desire."

Keep knocking on the doors of faith,
Ignore the noise, the unnecessary hate.
No one will truly get it,
Until the day you rise,
And become something great.
They may call it hocus pocus,
But never lose your focus.
Work hard in silence,
And let your success make the noise.
Yes, there will be times
When even you feel drained,
But remember, it's only you
Who can refill
Your endless desire to fulfill.

7. Give, Gain, Grow

"Give with purpose, grow with grace—consistency will lead you to your rightful place."

Find your reason to live,
And know it's always
Taking less and more to give.
What's truly yours will be yours,
When you give for a cause, not for applause.
Climb aboard the train of persistence,
Keep going, even through resistance.
Only then will you gain,
And drench yourself fully
In the success called rain.
Stay consistent,
Don't put on a show
Results will reflect,
As soon as you start to grow.

8. Hope, Happiness, Humor

"Turn the chaos into cheer—sometimes, a smile is all it takes to steer."

Turning hopelessness into hope,
Could there be anything dope?
Bringing people closer to their goal,
That's when you feel
Completely whole.
There's a lot of stress and tension,
The real world just doesn't pay attention.
At least for once, step out of the dizziness,
And do what brings you genuine happiness.
When rumours hover around,
Like a sticky tumour,
Turn things around
With your silly sense of humour.
Have a laugh, brighten your smile,
That's exactly what you need
To keep your mind agile.

9. Imagine, Improve, Inspire

"Your win begins within—ignite the fire, and let growth lead you to your own empire."

Imagine your win

It's not a sin.

It's a spark straight from your heart,

The very thing

That sets you apart.

It's not about a point to prove,

But to truly win,

You must improve.

Every step, every move

It's you who must approve.

Fuel the desire to inspire,

Keep alive that burning fire.

With every shift and changing gear,

Feel your success drawing near.

10. Joy, Journey, Jolly

*"Through every twist and turn, I choose to stay jolly—finding joy
even when life isn't all that holly."*

Cherish each moment with pure joy,
Like holding on to a childhood toy.
Whether it's night or day,
You just want to keep up the play.
It may sound a bit funny,
But isn't it all
Part of the journey?
Where even bittersweet learnings
Taste like honey.
Sure, life isn't always
A cute little lolly,
But through it all,
The only thing I wish for
Is to stay jolly.

11. Kick-start, Kidding, Kindness

"With the right ones by your side, even the wildest ride feels like home."

All set to kickstart your ride,
Ready to be blown away by the tide?
Well, absolutely not,
When you've got the right people
By your side.
The people who recognize your inner kid,
Never asking you to shut that lid.
They're always going to mine,
No matter how much you bid.
The harness to your kindness,
Such people are special,
The real deal,
Ones who are always
Going to be a part of your seal.

12. Love, Laugh, Live

"Love isn't just a feeling—it's the strength that teaches you to live, give, and grow through it all."

Love keeps you going,
Even when things aren't growing.
It tells you to never stop,
Even when you hit a drop.
It teaches you to laugh it off,
When things get rough.
Don't get me wrong,
That's exactly
What makes you tough.
It shows you that
It doesn't matter how much you give,
As long as you teach each other
How to live.

13. Mission, Magical, Memorable

"Trust your vision, embrace the spark—it's your magic that will leave a lasting mark."

Trust your vision,
Move ahead with precision,
Believe your decision,
Turn all of this into your life's mission.
Not everything requires you to be practical;
Some moments are special
Because you are magical.
You experience practicality's fusion
Only when you feel the spark of delusion.
Don't be afraid to be vulnerable
When things get miserable.
These are qualities that leave a mark,
If you want to be someone
Who always stays memorable.

14. Natural, Nurture, Nostalgia

"I don't claim to be intellectual, just someone expressing what feels natural—hoping my words bring peace, one moment at a time."

Don't think of myself as an intellectual,
I just keep expressing what feels natural,
With the hope that my words
Create a drastic change,
Even within the most minimal range.
Building a structure
Where one can naturally nurture,
Helping you explore happiness and well-being
In anything and everything
That feels worth giving.
Revealing the magic of nostalgia and memories,
Learning to slow down
When life isn't at ease,
To ultimately find a place
Where you feel at peace.

15. Observe, Obtain, Optimism

"Amidst the noise, let your sight guide you—retain what nurtures optimism and let it inspire others to believe."

All the things you preserve
Come with the ability to observe.
Finding what feels right,
Such is the power of your wonderful sight.
There's so much to obtain,
A long way to sustain,
So be mindful of
The things you choose to retain.
The world may overflow with pessimism,
But what sets you apart
Is the power to make someone believe
In the magic of optimism.

16. Patience, Passion, Perseverance

"Patience turns the journey into a masterpiece—let your actions speak louder than their judgments."

No one likes to wait,

We want every step to be straight,

But experiences teach us,

No matter the distance,

Enjoy the ride with patience.

With every action and reaction,

Just keep going in a never-ending fashion.

And if not now,

At least one day, the world shall realize

The true meaning of undying passion.

People will question your intelligence,

Talk about your negligence,

Judge you because of appearance,

Be prone to all this with tolerance.

Don't say anything until

They themselves see the wonders you create,

With your perseverance.

17. Quiet, Quirky, Quality

"Silence is powerful, humor is healing—value what truly matters, and abundance will follow."

Life got better
Once I understood
That silences are quite strong,
To get where you belong.
But amidst the chaos,
Always stay funny,
Be the one who's always quirky,
It's a great way to break the tension,
Even when you aren't the centre of attention.
The importance of quality over quantity,
Is a lesson all must learn.
Doesn't matter more or few,
Understand the value of this,
And you shall start receiving
More than you can ever earn.

18. Recognize, Refine, Recover

"Through the chaos, let your values be your guide—accept,
adapt, and rise each time you slide."

It takes a while to realize,
Not everything is glittery and nice.
You must make a choice
And pick a side of all the values you
Carry along the ride.
Yes, things never stay in line,
And a lot changes with time.
Acceptance and adaptation are all you seek
If you're looking for ways to refine.
New lessons you will always discover,
As many things shall throw you off guard.
But your values will help you recover,
Even when you fall down hard.

19. Selective, Sincere, Special

*"Choose with confidence, trust your potential, and let sincerity
be the key to your influence and essence."*

Your mind is constantly on the loose,

When there are wide options to choose.

Pick what feels effective

Trust me,

It's okay to be selective.

Believe what you want is already here,

But remember, it's just as important

To stay sincere.

As you draw near,

It's natural to carry a gentle fear.

Recognize what's essential,

Trust your potential,

Be someone influential.

That's exactly what

Makes you truly special.

20. Train, Thrive, Triumph

"Growth thrives in the willingness to learn—embrace the journey, and happiness will follow, unforced and true."

Learning something new
Might feel like a pain,
But there's no growth
If you don't carry
The spark to train.
It's not about if you can survive,
But about
The willingness to thrive.
After all, in this vehicle called life,
It's you who has to drive.
Facing defeats along the way,
That's what adds thrills to this ride.
Trying to be happy is all a bluff,
But truly being happy,
There lies my real triumph.

21. Unicorns, Unique, Unconditional

*"Let your imagination be limitless—where every dream is free,
and every thought is unconditionally yours."*

Living in your rosy world
Is never wrong.
Dream of flying through unicorns,
While rainbows play a magical song.
The real world is hard,
And everything you do meets critique,
But this world you've made for yourself
Needs none,
That's what makes it unique.
Everyone might call it crazy,
Madness, or delusion.
But set no boundaries to your thoughts,
Go all out with imagination.
After all, it's the only place where
Anything you give or take
Feels truly unconditional.

22. Vision, Value, Victory

"Respect the vision of others, nurture your own, and value those who uplift you even before the world sees your crown."

Yes, I understand,
Your story is led by your vision.
But it's also important to
Respect others' decisions,
As not everything you do
Shall meet the right precision.
Respect and value other thoughts,
When you experience creative droughts.
The shower of ideas helps your mind to bloom,
Giving you a sense of direction,
Rather than believing
In the things you assume.
Be mindful of those you welcome
Into your inventory,
Not everyone will
Celebrate your victory.
Cherish the ones who helped you rise,
Even before your success,
These are your biggest prize.

23. Wish, Warmth, Wholesome

*"Stay true, keep growing, and be the reason for someone's
joy—this is the art that makes life truly fulfilling."*

Be the reason for someone's smile,
Keep growing while staying juvenile.
You might not always know the ingredients
Of this special dish,
But to savour its pleasant taste,
There's no better wish.
It brings out such warmth within you,
Knowing you're among the fortunate few.
Repeating tasks time and again,
Yet managing to create
Something fresh and new.
After all, it's not easy to stay true to yourself,
In a world that's often gruesome.
But never let go of this feeling,
The art of making things wholesome.
Realize that this is what
Truly makes you awesome.

24. Xylophone: Melodiously Colorful

"Life is a symphony of seasons—embrace the highs, the lows, and craft your own melody along the way."

The reason I chose this,
Is solely due to the reason,
That just like its colourful tunes,
Our lives go through
Several melodious seasons.
You encounter various tones,
As life carries you
Through countless zones,
Ultimately creating a unique song
Called life,
A melody you can call your own.
Glide through the magic,
Stride through the tragic.
Even if you don't follow
A certain path shown,
You'll still find a way
To create your own xylophone.

25. YOLO, Yippee, Yours

"Fear may hold you back, but the voice inside knows when it's time to soar. Trust it, and you'll always find your way back to your true self."

When fear strikes,
And your inner voice hides,
Buddy, what's the fear?
Just go for it,
After all— "YOLO."
Alright, I get it,
You Only Live Once,
But that doesn't mean I act like a hippie.
I can't just jump into everything,
Shouting "yippee."
The voice then responds:
Sure, we're not here to force.
You're free to close these doors.
But remember,
We speak only when we mean it.
You might step back now,
But later, when things fall in place,
You'll realize it was still us,
Who nudged you to take that step,
To spread those wings.
One way or another,
You always keep us close.
Because no matter what,

We will always be yours.

26. Zen, Zesty, Zealous

"Embrace your journey with zest and zeal, for the path you've carved is uniquely yours, and the only way forward is through self-belief and the lessons you've learned."

You've come so far,
Managed to create your own den.
Now step back a little,
And embrace your well-deserved zen.
Zestiness brought you here,
Propelling you forward.
Savor it all,
Conquer your fears,
While keeping your values near.
Why be jealous,
When you can choose
To be zealous?
To some, this might sound ridiculous,
But hold everything you've learned
In both your mind and heart,
And you'll truly embark
On the path to being
Someone fabulous.

Closure

Hope this was a wonderful read and has brought about some positive change in your life.

I understand that life isn't always rosy and often presents many challenges, but if we train ourselves and cultivate a stronger mindset, we can face any obstacle with a smile.

In the end, everything works out, and we have the power to build lives that are meaningful and memorable.

Wishing you all the best, and I hope you carry and spread the joy of this message to as many people as possible, for this is the need of the hour.

"The world needs more empathy and less judgment."

www.ingramcontent.com/pod-product-compliance
Lightning Source LLC
Chambersburg PA
CBHW022228160726

47991CB00016B/2644